What do we think about

Bullying?

Jillian Powell

WAYLAND

Titles in the series
What do we think about
Alcohol   **Disability**

Bullying   **Drugs**

Death   **Family Break-Up**

 See page 31 for ways in which you can use this book to encourage literacy skills.

Editors: Carron Brown and Kim Protheroe
Consultant: John Bennett, a Health Education Coordinator
Cover designer: Jan Sterling
Designer: Jean Wheeler
Photo stylist: Gina Brown
Production controller: Carol Titchener

First published in 1998 by Wayland Publishers Limited,
61 Western Road, Hove, East Sussex BN3 1JD

British Library Cataloguing in Publication Data
Powell, Jillian
What do we think about bullying?
1. Bullying – Juvenile literature
I. Title II. Bullying
371.5'8

ISBN 0 7502 2207 7

Picture acknowledgements
All photographs by Martyn F. Chillmaid.
The photographer and the publishers would like to thank the staff, parents and pupils of St Stephen's First School, Redditch, who acted out the scenes and assisted with the photography in this book.

Printed and bound by Eurografica S.p.A. in Vicenza, Italy

Contents

What is bullying?

Shouting at someone – that's bullying.

Calling people names – that's bullying.

Talking behind someone's back, taking or
spoiling their things, hitting or pushing
someone around, touching them in a way
that makes them feel afraid or unhappy –
that's all bullying.

What is a bully?

A bully can be a girl or a boy, an adult or a child.

Anyone who tries to hurt or upset someone, or make him or her feel small or unhappy, is a bully.

There are bullies at school and bullies at home.

What do bullies want?

Bullies want to feel big and important.

They want to feel that they are better than other people.

They want to hurt other people and make them feel small.

That's why getting upset or even crying is giving bullies what they want.

Who gets bullied?

Anyone can get bullied.

People can get bullied for being big or small, rich or poor.

They can be bullied for the way they look or talk.

Bullies often pick on people because they are different in some way.
But everyone is different.

It is never your fault if you get bullied.

How do bullies feel?

Bullies often feel unhappy inside.
Sometimes they are jealous of others, so
they try to upset them and spoil their fun.

Sometimes bullies have
been hurt or bullied
themselves.

John's brother bullied him at home. John didn't like being picked on. It made him feel horrible. At school, he picked on smaller children. It made John feel strong and important when people were afraid of him.

How does it feel to be bullied?

Being bullied can make people feel afraid and lonely, angry or upset.

Fiona felt too afraid to say she was scared of meeting the bullies.

Being bullied gave Fiona nightmares.
She found it very hard to get to sleep.
Some nights she didn't sleep at all.

Fiona thought that it was her fault
that she was being bullied.

Where do people get bullied?

People get bullied in school corridors, in toilets and changing rooms, in the classroom or in the playground, behind walls or at home.

Bullies pick places where they can
get someone alone, so they won't
get caught.

Why don't people tell on bullies?

It can feel scary to tell on a bully.

Karim thought the bullying would get worse if he got the bully into trouble.

Karim thought about telling his teacher, but he was scared that she would say it was all his own fault. He was also afraid that she might tell him to stop complaining and fight back.

What makes bullying worse?

Bullying gets worse when bullies get away with it.

They get away with it when people are afraid to tell on them.

Fighting back can make bullying worse, too.
You can get hurt by fighting a bully.

How can bullying be stopped?

If someone starts bullying you,
try to stay with other people so
that the bully can't get you alone.

If a bully tries to make you do something you don't want to do, say 'No' firmly and walk away.

If a bully hits or kicks you, try to get away from him or her and get help.

Why should you tell on a bully?

Telling on a bully isn't telling tales.
Bullies must be stopped if they are
making someone else unhappy.
Bullies are often unhappy too and
they need help.

Clare knew it was important to tell
someone about being bullied. The
bullies would have carried on bullying
if Clare hadn't told her teacher about
them. Her teacher said that she could
help stop the bullying.

Who can help?

If you are being bullied, tell an adult you can trust. It could be someone who cares for you or a teacher at school. If they don't help you, find someone who will.

It can help to talk to friends, too. Joining a group or club where you will meet new friends can make you feel stronger and better.

Notes for parents and teachers

Use this book as a basis for children's knowledge about bullies and bullying. Ask a group of children why they think people bully. Then ask them how they think bullying makes people feel. Try a role-play situation where a group of children headed by a bully confronts a child. Ask the two characters how they felt during the role-play and work on the feelings they produced.

Mention self-esteem, and how it is important that all children should feel good about themselves and what they do. Ask them about what makes them feel good, such as having fun with your friends. Talk about why having good friends is important, what makes a good friend, and where to make friends (clubs and groups). Happy children do not make bullies and tend not to be bullied.

Talk about the places where people get bullied. Ask the children how they think the places could be made safer. Suggestions could include travelling around in groups, and teachers patrolling the corridors and playgrounds.

Talk about who the children can go to to tell on a bully. Talk about how important it is to tell on a bully and how to make people listen. Emphasise how important it is to tell someone you trust if you are unhappy. Maybe a teacher whom the children trust can be appointed to deal specifically with problems relating to bullying. Mention the free helpline run by Childline.

Glossary

Jealous Wanting to have the things someone else has, or to be like them.

Spoil To mess something up or damage it.

Trust When you know someone cares for you and will help you.

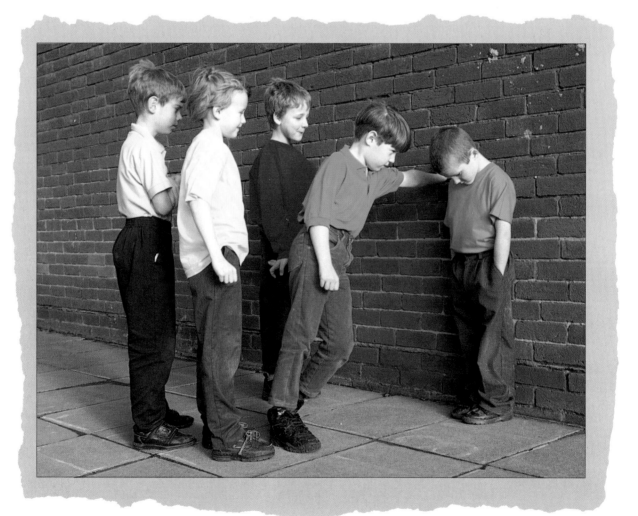

Further information

Books to read

Let's Talk About Bullying by Angela Grunsell (Watts, 1995)

How do I feel about Bullies and Gangs? by Julie Johnson (Watts, 1996)

'Stop That!' An Anti-Bullying Rap by Lorraine Simeon and Rowan Clifford (Blackie, 1994)

Organizations that support people include:

Kidscape (Campaign for Children's Safety)
152 Buckingham Palace Road, London SW1W 9TR
Tel: 0171 730 3300

Anti-Bullying Campaign (ABC)
10 Borough High Street, London SE1 9QQ
Tel: 0171 378 1446

Childline
Free helpline: 0800 1111

Use this book for teaching literacy

This book can help you in the literacy hour in the following ways:

✓ Children can use the book's contents page, page numbers, headings and index to locate a particular piece of information.

✓ They can use the glossary to reinforce their alphabetic knowledge and extend their vocabulary.

✓ They can compare this book with fictional stories about bullying to show how similar information can be presented in different ways.

✓ They can try rewriting some of the situations described in the form of a story.

Index